W9-BLV-567

Gorillas

SEYMOUR SIMON

HarperCollins*Publishers*

GORILLAS are sometimes called *anthropoid* (manlike) apes. A gorilla has two arms and two legs, and a head and body much like a human's head and body. A gorilla also has five fingers and five toes, and thirty-two teeth. You have all of those too, and twenty-eight teeth, in about the same positions. Of course, gorillas are much hairier than people. An adult gorilla has hair all over its body except for its face, its chest, and the palms of its hands and soles of its feet.

Gorillas are almost nothing like the scary beasts you see in Hollywood movies. Real gorillas don't snatch humans and carry them off into the jungle. They do not climb tall buildings and swat planes from the sky. Gorillas in nature are shy, secretive animals. If you go to a zoo and see a gorilla face-to-face, it feels as if the gorilla is watching you with as much interest and wonder as you are watching it. The more you find out about gorillas, the more interesting and less fearsome they become.

All gorillas live in a few heavily forested areas in Africa. Scientists have divided them into three groups, or subspecies. Most of the gorillas you see in zoos or museums are western lowland gorillas (scientific name: *Gorilla gorilla gorilla*). As many as 100,000 live in the tropical rain forests of west Africa. Fully grown western lowland gorillas vary in size from one to another, but they are still quite huge compared to you. A western lowland gorilla's body hair is usually short and ranges in color from black to grayish brown.

The eastern lowland gorilla (*Gorilla gorilla graueri*), shown here, lives in the rain forests of central Africa, about six hundred miles east of the western lowland gorilla and across the Congo River. There are fewer than two dozen eastern gorillas living in captivity and probably only several thousand living in the wild today. They are a bit larger than their western relatives, and they have darker hair color and slightly longer jaws and teeth.

The mountain gorilla (*Gorilla gorilla beringei*), shown here, is the largest of all three kinds. Fully grown males may weigh more than four hundred pounds, about the weight of ten second-grade children. They also have broader chests, wider feet and hands, and the longest jaws and teeth. The head of a mountain gorilla is often higher and more pointed than the head of a lowland gorilla. A mountain gorilla has a wider gap in the middle of its nose, and its forearms are shorter than those of the other kinds of gorillas.

Mountain gorillas live in the Virunga Mountains of the African countries of the Democratic Republic of Congo, Rwanda, and Uganda. The word "virunga" means "a lonely mountain that reaches the clouds." Cloud forests in the Virungas are quite cool. The dark body hair of a mountain gorilla is long and helps keep it warm.

Mountain gorillas are the rarest of all gorillas. Only a few hundred live in two separate patches of forest. None live in zoos.

Many of a gorilla's bones and muscles are like yours. But the arms are much longer, and the chest, shoulders, neck, and head are much larger and heavier than yours. A gorilla also has a much bigger stomach than you do. It needs a big stomach to hold all the plants it eats every day.

A gorilla uses its hands and fingers to hold objects. Its fingers have fingernails and fingerprints that look like humans' prints, only larger.

Gorillas have bigger and more powerful muscles in their arms than in their legs. They can stand erect, but they walk on all fours using their arms as front legs and curling their fingers underneath. When they knuckle walk, their knuckles support their body weight. Gorillas often travel slowly, but they can also trot or even canter like a horse to move quickly.

Baby gorillas weigh only four to five pounds when they are born. A newborn baby has a very powerful grip and clings tightly to the hair on its mother's stomach. When it gets older, it will ride on her back when she travels.

Baby gorillas have a lot of growing to do, and they start very fast. They can do many physical things before human babies can do them. Baby gorillas begin crawling in their second month. After a few more months they begin to stand and walk. Human babies usually start crawling later, at seven months. By the end of the first year human babies begin to develop their use of language and speech. Baby gorillas learn to communicate more slowly and in different ways.

Like human children young gorillas spend a lot of time playing. They do somersaults, climb trees, and slide down hills on their stomachs. They pretend play at biting, chasing, tackling, and wrestling. They seem to have an all-around grand time.

Gorillas often live in small family groups each headed by a silverback, a large adult male. The rest of the family consists of a few blackbacks—younger, smaller males—and several females and their youngsters. As a male gorilla grows older and heavier, the hair on his back slowly turns gray, much like the hair on an older person's head. By the time a male has taken command of a family, his back hair may be totally gray.

A silverback is heavily built, weighing more than four hundred pounds and possibly as much as six hundred pounds. He stands five and a half feet tall or more and has an arm spread of eight feet, about the distance from the floor to the ceiling in a house. Despite his huge size, he is patient with the playful youngsters in his family. He allows them to cling to him and pull his hair.

Gorillas in families eat together, groom each other, and play together under the protection of the silverback male or males. A gorilla family can contain anywhere from two to thirty-five individuals. Usually, though, there are five to ten members in a family.

The silverback decides which way to travel to find food, where the family will stop to rest, and where it will sleep each evening. When families travel, the silverback often leads, followed by the blackbacks and the females with their young. It seems every gorilla knows its place in the order of the family, and there is only occasional fighting.

When blackbacks become silverbacks, they may leave the group and travel alone or stay and help fight off intruders. When young females grow up, they leave to join other males or other families.

Gorillas spend much of the day feeding in open, sunny sections of the forest that are just growing back after a fire or a storm. When feeding, gorillas space themselves out so that they are not on top of each other. They eat juicy fruits, leaves, stems, and shoots. A four-hundred-pound gorilla can eat up to fifty pounds of plants a day. The plants contain so much water that gorillas rarely need open water for drinking.

A gorilla can use its feet to grab plants or shake fruit, the most favored food, from a tree. Females and young gorillas can pick fruit on thin branches that are unreachable by the heavier males. A large male gorilla may climb a tree to reach a favorite snack.

Gorillas are awkward climbers. They use both their hands and feet when they go up a tree. They rarely jump from branch to branch the way monkeys do. Gorillas come down from a tree slowly in reverse, hind feet first, carefully checking branches all the way to the ground.

In the early-morning sunlight of a jungle clearing, a family of gorillas searches for food, belching and murmuring softly to each other. The silverback belches and keeps them together. When alarmed, he may produce a short bark to speed them along.

Around midday, when the sun is at the highest point, the group stops for a rest. The silverback chooses a spot, and the others lie down around him. If the grasses are very high, each gorilla beats them flat. This creates a more comfortable resting place and also allows a better view of the surroundings.

The gorillas sit and doze for a moment or two. Then they start to groom themselves and others. They use their fingers, lips, and eyes to examine and clean their skin, hair, and nails. A mother cleans her baby by holding it in one hand and grooming with the other hand. Sometimes young gorillas groom the silverback. This helps the silverback bond with them. After a while the adults slowly drift off to sleep while the young gorillas play. A more peaceful scene is hard to imagine.

In the early afternoon the silverback awakens. The gorillas stir, stretch, and move on. They eat and wander until shortly before nighttime. They bed down to sleep in individual nests either on the ground or on the lower branches of trees.

Gorillas use several sounds and facial expressions to let other gorillas know what they are thinking or feeling. One of the most common is a tight-lip expression. The gorilla tilts its head downward, tucks its lips into a tight line, and gives another gorilla an angry stare. It may hoot at this time, or beat its chest. When a gorilla opens its mouth, just showing its lower teeth, then it's relaxed and content. But when it bares its upper as well as lower teeth, watch out! The gorilla is tense and threatening you.

Here are a number of sounds gorillas make and what the sounds mean: An infant will shriek when it is bothered or separated from its mother. That will bring the mother back to the infant quickly. A chuckle is often used during social play. A kind of a hiccup or question bark means slight alarm or curiosity. A gorilla belch means that it is feeding contentedly or sleeping nicely. One gorilla belches, and soon all the gorillas are belching in a slow, relaxing chorus.

Male gorillas use sounds and body language to show that they are annoyed or angry at another gorilla in the family or at an intruder. A silverback usually needs only to roar once to send the message. But if that doesn't work, the male bares his teeth and walks on his hind legs in a kind of a strut, holding his upper body erect and stretching his arms outward.

He may begin to beat his chest loudly and excitedly. The gorilla cups his hand and brings it down with force against his chest, making a loud *pock-pock* sound. The silverback may beat his chest to move family members along, to stop fights that may arise between them, or to attract the females' attention. A male gorilla may start beating his chest at the sight of an intruder (that's you if you get too close).

Chest beating is a way a gorilla shows his strength while avoiding an actual attack. If chest beating doesn't do the trick, the gorilla may charge forward as a threat. From a standing position or from a stiff, elbows-out, knuckles-on-the-ground stance, the male begins to hoot faster and faster. He shakes a nearby tree, tears out a shrub, or picks up some rocks and throws them into the air.

Finally the male charges. In the bluff charge he runs sideways back and forth past the intruder or another male. In the rush charge the male runs directly at his adversary, usually stopping just short of a collision, but sometimes the gorilla makes contact with the object of his anger.

Usually the only contact is a shouldering aside or a smack. Rarely does a gorilla actually start fighting at the end of a charge. An all-out fight between males occurs only when the silverback is challenged for his leadership by another silverback.

A male gorilla who wants to show the silverback that he isn't interested in challenging him will move out of the way or retreat. Gorillas are not violent animals. When they scare an intruder or a rival gorilla away, they don't follow and try to kill it. Instead, they turn and walk back peacefully to their family.

Gorillas don't reproduce quickly. The female gives birth to a single baby only once every three to five years. Gorillas have no natural enemies. Even a lion or leopard usually would not dare to attack them. The natural life span of a gorilla may be more than forty, or even as much as fifty, years. So the numbers of gorillas remain fairly constant from year to year, except when gorillas come up against people who harm them in some way. Then the numbers of gorillas can drop quickly and dangerously.

Mountain gorillas are the most endangered gorilla subspecies. Like so many other wild animals, they are being forced from their ancient forests to make way for humans who wish to farm, lumber, and build homes. Civil wars in the region have made it even more difficult to find out what's happening to the gorillas living in the Virunga Mountains.

Zoos and museums have stopped taking gorillas from the wild. But poachers continue to hunt down these great, shy animals. Gorilla poaching is a crime, but it will go on as long as some thoughtless people are willing to pay large amounts of money for bushmeat, gorilla trophies, or baby gorillas to be raised as pets. To capture a baby gorilla, poachers will kill the entire family as the members rush to defend the infant.

George Schaller was the first scientist to study gorillas in the wild, in the late 1950s. Later, Dian Fossey spent twenty years, from 1966 to 1985, studying mountain gorillas. Books and films such as *Gorillas in the Mist* have helped us learn about gorilla family life and behavior and become sympathetic to the plight of gorillas. The key to their survival is to preserve the forests they live in and to protect them from hunters and poachers.

Several organizations around the world are working to improve the odds of gorillas surviving in the wild. In their view, the key is to train and pay local people to help in the conservation effort.

Gorillas and humans share ninety-eight percent of their DNA, the chemical substance that makes each animal unique and special. If you gaze into the eyes of a gorilla and think how human it looks, you won't be far wrong! Clearly, the fate of gorillas is up to humans. If we can give them the chance to be left alone in their natural surroundings, gorillas may well be able to survive and perhaps even increase in numbers.

To Joel, Benjamin, Chloe, and Jeremy

—From Grandpa with love

Gorillas
Copyright © 2000 by Seymour Simon
Printed in the U.S.A. All rights reserved. www.harperchildrens.com

Library of Congress Cataloging-in-Publication Data
Simon, Seymour.
  Gorillas / Seymour Simon.
    p.   cm.
  Summary: Describes the physical characteristics and behavior of various kinds of gorillas.
  ISBN 0-06-023035-5. — ISBN 0-06-023036-3 (lib. bdg.)
  1. Gorilla—Juvenile literature. [1. Gorilla.] I. Title.
QL737.P96 S56 2000   99-087161
599.884—dc21   CIP
                                           AC

Typography by Elynn Cohen   2 3 4 5 6 7 8 9 10 ❖ First Edition